Daddy, Is there really a God?

WRITTEN BY:
JOHN D. MORRIS

ILLUSTRATED BY:
Jonathan Chong

M3
Master
Books

First Printing, July 1997
Second Printing, December 2000

For information write: Master Books, Inc., P.O. Box 727, Green Forest, AR 72638

ISBN: 0-89051-188-8
Library of Congress: 97-73935

Master
Books

Dedication

This "nearly true" story is dedicated to my oldest daughter, Chara, whose name comes from the New Testament Greek word for joy. Chara has always made careful "observations" and frequently asks her father tough questions.

Hi, boys and girls, my name is Tracker John, and this is my little dinosaur friend, D.J. He is a psittacosaurs (sit-uh-cuh-SAWR-us), a dinosaur with a nose which reminds you of a parrot's beak. I work at the Institute for Creation Research. Scientists here at ICR study about God's creation. We can learn a lot about God and the Bible from the things God has made.

Recently, we left on a field trip with several families to do just that — learn more about God's creation. We camped out for several days.

Some scientists don't believe in God. They think that everything, like plants and animals, just happened, with no help from God. They think that each type of plant and animal came from some other type of plant or animal. They don't "observe" things like that happening, that's just what they think. The name for this idea is evolution (e-vol-U-shun).

Scientists at ICR study plants and animals, too. But the ICR scientists are Christians. We believe in God and His Word, the Bible. When we study plants and animals and the world, we find reasons to believe that God *did* create them, just like the Bible says.

On our field trip, we studied plants and animals. We even studied fossil plants and animals. We saw fossil wood and leaves. We studied fossils of sea animals, like clams, even though the ocean was far away.

Once the sun went down, we studied tiny plants and animals under the microscope. We made many good observations on each one.

One night around the campfire after we had prayed, one little girl, Joy, asked her father and me some very serious questions. "How do I know there really is a God? I've never seen Him. How can I be sure?"

"How can I even know about creation? My friend next door — her teacher believes in evolution. She says everything just happened with no God at all! How am I supposed to know?"

Questions are very good things. That's how we learn. Scientists are always asking questions. Sometimes, no one knows the answers to the questions. To get the answers, they must study very hard and make good "observations."

Joy is always making good observations. Every time we go on group hikes she "observes" things and asks me questions. Whenever she comes to ICR, she observes the experiments and asks the scientists questions. Maybe someday she'll make a good scientist, too.

This question was a very important question. She needed a good answer. We all need a good answer to this question.

So, before I said anything, I prayed in my heart to God that He would give her dad and me wisdom in our answer.

After we talked, her father and I decided not to just tell Joy the answer, but to let her make some good observations and answer the questions herself. I promised to do a set of experiments with her in a few days, at the end of our field trip.

For the next several days, Joy watched D.J. and me getting ready. She got more and more excited each day. How would the question be answered?

Before we started, I reminded Joy how in the beginning God had created the earth, plants, animals, and people. No persons were there to observe creation, but He has told us about it in the Bible.

Today, we can observe the things He created so long ago. Since God created all things, we ought to be able to see that creation couldn't just happen by itself.

As an example, we talked about things humans make. Can we tell the difference between something somebody made and something that just happened? What observations can we make to help us decide?

For example, look at this lump of clay. It doesn't look like anything.

But, a person can take that lump and shape it into something that they want — like a flower vase or a coffee cup. Even if you didn't "observe" it being made you know that somebody made it.

"How can you tell the difference between something that somebody made and something that just happened?" I asked her. "What observations can you make to help you decide?"

Tracker John," Joy said, "things that someone makes would have a certain shape. It wouldn't just be a blob. And when people make something, they want to use it for some reason, like holding flowers or drinking coffee. Sometimes things people make have more than one part, and the parts work together — like the microscope. Each part does its job.

"Or, how about a book?" she continued. "The letters on the page spell out words that we can understand. That doesn't just happen! Or how about this picture in the book? Somebody drew this picture on purpose! Not only that, but it takes a lot of people doing lots of different jobs before a book is ready to read. It's easy to decide if something just happened or if someone did it on purpose."

"Okay," I said, "let's look in the sacks."

Author - Writes

Artist - Designs

Pressman - Prints

Sack number one had pieces of wood in it. Some were just pieces of tree bark and others were twigs from a bush behind the tent. "Nobody made these," she said.

Next, Joy took out a wooden button. She knew what that was for. "Somebody made that," she said. Then she found a wooden stick. She wasn't real sure what it was used for, but she knew someone had made it. I explained that doctors use these to hold down your tongue when they look at your throat.

A wood carving of a dinosaur was easy. D.J. laughed because it looked like a friend of his.

"Even if I don't know what something is for, I can tell if somebody made it," she decided.

17

Joy was surprised when she opened sack number two. It was just a stack of paper! "Look carefully," I said. The first piece of paper had nothing on it, and the next just had a few ink spots scattered all over the page. "Somebody may have done this, but they didn't do it on purpose," remarked Joy.

But then there was a page with some scribbling on it. "That's not very pretty, but somebody did it," said Joy. "It couldn't just happen."

Next was a newspaper in a different language. "I don't know what it says, but it says something," Joy pointed out.

Finally, she picked out a written note from her father. It said:

Your mother and I love you very much,
and so does Tracker John.
We want you to keep asking
questions and finding the answers.

We know that as you do,
you will grow in the wisdom
and knowledge of the Lord.

Love,
Dad

"I love you, too, Dad," Joy said as she gave him a hug. "I get the point. Words and sentences must be written by someone on purpose. I can read the words and I know what they mean. That couldn't be an accident."

Sack number three had many things in it. Some were just regular old rocks. They had no special shape at all. Then Joy found a rock with a fossil sea creature in it. She had found the fossil earlier that day. She observed its shape, noticed it had a shell, and studied the markings on the shell. She could tell where the two parts of the shell had been held together by a muscle.

"The rock is just a rock," Joy observed, "but the animal looks like somebody made it."

The fossil looked just like living clams she had seen. Even though the fossil was stone, it had been alive once. *It had to have been created,* she thought, *the same for the fossil fish, too.*

The same was true for the nautilus fossil. It had been cut open with a saw. Joy could see many "rooms" inside where the creature had lived. She remembered the nautilus shell she had back home. Its shape looked just the same, but it had not turned to stone. It had the same "rooms." Its shell had such beautiful colors, it was used as a decoration. "Nothing so beautiful and with so many parts working together could happen by chance," she decided.

"But who made them?" I asked. "Did a person make the fish?"

"No," she answered, "a person might make the shape and paint the colors, but they wouldn't be alive."

The last sack was heavy, for it had a science textbook and a computer CD in it. They had many beautiful pictures of plants and animals.

The school textbook showed how each living thing is made up of organs, like the heart and stomach. The organs — the muscles, the blood, the bones, and everything else are made up of tiny cells. There are many different kinds of cells. There are skin cells, blood cells, teeth cells, heart cells — every kind of cell.

Inside each tiny cell are many teeny-tiny organs. Each one has a special job to do, and they all work together to make the cell work. Without each one the cell would die. Even the skin covering the cell has many parts, all doing their jobs. Hundreds of parts doing hundreds of jobs — all of them inside each little cell.

The bigger the plant or animal the more cells are in their bodies and the more different kinds of cells. A person is made up of hundreds and thousands and millions and billions and trillions of cells — all working together!

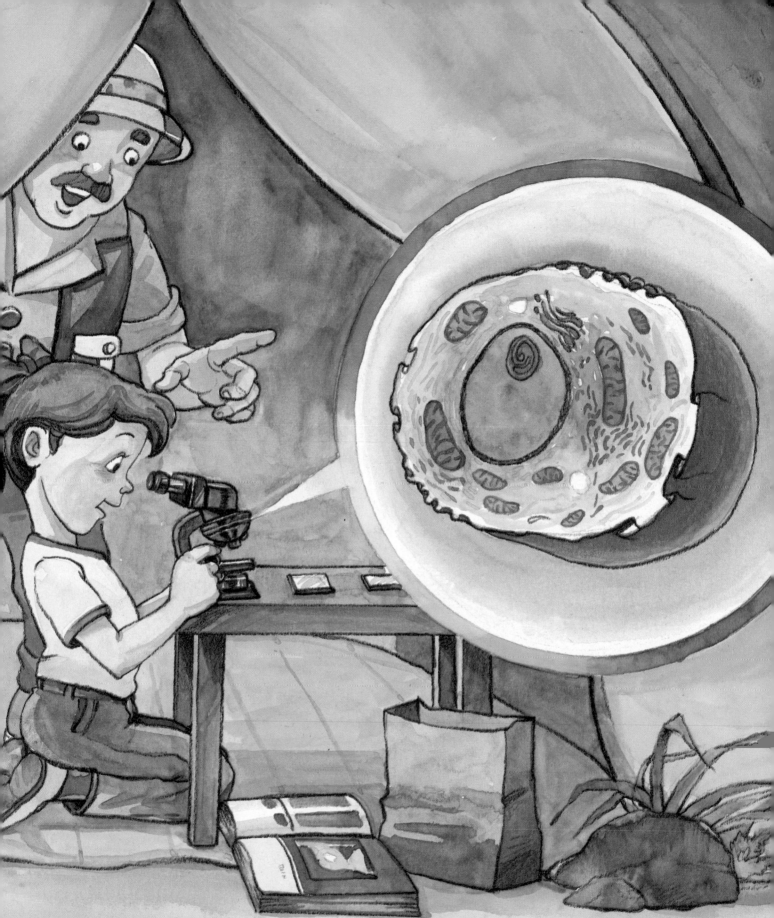

It reminded Joy of a computer, but with many more parts. She knew it took a whole group of very smart scientists to make a computer, and a computer is not even alive. It's just a machine.

"Each living cell would be harder to make than a computer. No way could it just happen!" she exclaimed. "Someone smarter than a person had to make cells and then He had to make it alive. The maker had to be alive and able to give life, too."

23

The computer CD explained that each cell contained written instructions in a language the rest of the cell could read and understand. This long stringy "book of instructions" would be over a mile long if you could stretch it out. Scientists call this message the "DNA code."

The DNA in each cell tells the cell how to grow and what to do. It tells the cell whether to be a part of the brain or part of a finger. When a human baby is growing inside the mother's womb it tells it to grow ten fingers and ten toes and one nose. It explains where the heart will be and shows the muscles how to make it beat. It knows if the child is to have red hair or blond, blue eyes or brown. Maybe he or she will be tall, maybe short. The DNA knows it all. It's like a book. Even a single cell has more written information than the biggest library in the world. "Where did all this information come from?" I asked.

Joy didn't even have to think about it, "Books don't get written all by themselves. And the DNA couldn't just happen. It couldn't write itself. Someone very smart had to write the DNA code!" I asked her to think carefully, "Who could write the DNA code? Who could create living things? Who could make them come alive?"

"No human scientist can create a living cell," Joy answered. "They really can't make a person. There must be a God! Only He is powerful enough and smart enough, and He is alive, so He can give life!"

These things are all true. You've made some good observations," I said. "Only God can create life. But there is much more we can know about God. God is also holy. He never sins. In fact, sin breaks His heart. He can never allow sin or anyone who sins to be with Him in heaven. But He also loves us, and He wants us to love Him, too, and live with Him in heaven. He created us to behave in a way that would please Him, and it breaks His heart when we choose to do wrong. This is called sin, and we all sin sometimes. Maybe we disobey our parents, or treat someone mean. Maybe we tell a lie. It's all sin. The Bible tells us that the punishment for sin is death — death forever — in a place far away from God and His love.

So do you know what God did? God sent His only son, Jesus Christ, to die on the cross for our sins. He was punished instead of us. And then the Creator of life rose from the dead to offer us forgiveness of our sins and eternal life. Now we can be washed clean of our sins and live forever with Him."

"How can we know this is true?" Joy asked.

"Well, we didn't observe it, but many people did. They told us about it in the Bible," I replied. "You remember, at first you didn't know if there really was a God. Now, from the observations you made, you're sure there is a God, just like the Bible says. Then, you had questions about the Bible story of creation, and now you know that nothing else makes sense. Creation has got to be true. Things can't happen by chance. We can be sure that what the Bible says is true. In just the same way, we know what the Bible says about forgiveness is also true. God will forgive your sins when you ask Him to, and make you His dear child."

Remember, everyone sins, even children sin, and break God's heart. To be forgiven, we must ask God to forgive us, because Jesus Christ has already been punished for our sins on the cross. We must truly be sorry for our sins — sorry that we broke God's heart. But we also know that He still loves us and hears our prayers. He will gladly forgive us when we ask Him to."

When you are older there may be other times when you have questions. Questions like: "Am I really a Christian?" "Did God really forgive my sins?" "Am I really going to heaven?"

Whenever the questions come, just remember what you know. Creation is true. This world and living things could not just happen. There must be a God, just like the Bible says. We can believe everything else the Bible says, too, even about sin and forgiveness. At the times of questions, just remember and then thank God for teaching you about creation, and for forgiving you and making you His child. As you thank Him, the questions will be answered.

For God so loved the world, that He gave His only begotten Son,
that whosoever believeth in Him should not perish,
but have everlasting life (John 3:16).

Well, boys and girls, we had quite an adventure, didn't we? With Joy's help, we learned that creation is true, that the Bible is true, and that there really *is* a God. Finally, we learned that the Creator is also our Saviour, who died for our sins. Please join D.J. and me for the next creation adventure!

Scriptures About Creation

In the beginning God created the heaven and the earth (Gen. 1:1).

So God created man in His own image, in the image of God created He him; male and female created He them (Gen. 1:27).

And God saw everything that He had made, and behold, it was very good. And the evening and the morning were the sixth day (Gen 1:31).

For in six days the Lord made heaven and earth, the sea, and all that in them is, and rested the seventh day: wherefore the Lord blessed the Sabbath day, and hallowed it (Exod. 20:11).

I will praise thee; for I am fearfully and wonderfully made: marvelous are thy works; and that my soul knoweth right well. My substance was not hid from thee, when I was made in secret, and curiously wrought in the lowest parts of the earth. Thine eyes did see my substance, yet being unperfect; and in thy book all my members were written, which in continuance were fashioned, when as yet there was none of them (Ps. 139:14-16).

For the invisible things of Him from the creation of the world are clearly seen, being understood by the things that are made, even His eternal power and Godhead; so that they are without excuse (Rom. 1:20).

For by Him were all things created, that are in heaven, and that are in earth, visible, and invisible, whether they be thrones, or dominions, or principalities, or powers: all things were created by Him, and for Him (Col. 1:16).

Thou art worthy, O Lord, to receive glory and honor and power: for thou hast created all things, and for thy pleasure they are and were created (Rev. 4:11).

Scriptures About Salvation

As it is written, There is none righteous, no, not one (Rom. 3:10).

For all have sinned, and come short of the glory of God (Rom. 3:23).

Wherefore, as by one man sin entered into the world, and death by sin; and so death passed upon all men, for that all have sinned (Rom 5:12).

For the wages of sin is death; but the gift of God is eternal life through Jesus Christ our Lord (Rom 6:23).

But God commendeth His love toward us, in that, while we were yet sinners, Christ died for us (Rom 5:8).

For whosoever shall call upon the name of the Lord shall be saved (Rom 10:13).

If thou shalt confess with thy mouth the Lord Jesus, and shalt believe in thine heart that God hath raised Him from the dead, thou shalt be saved. For with the heart man believeth unto righteousness; and with the mouth confession is made unto salvation (Rom. 10:9-10).

Recommended Reading

What Really Happened to the Dinosaurs?
by John D. Morris and Ken Ham
(Green Forest, AR: Master Books, 1988), 32 pgs.

Noah's Ark and the Ararat Adventure
by John D. Morris
(Green Forest, AR: Master Books, 1994), 64 pgs.

Dry Bones and Other Fossils
By Gary Parker
(Green Forest, AR: Master Books, 1995), 80 pgs.

Life Before Birth
by Gary Parker
(Green Forest, AR: Master Books, 1992), 88 pgs.

A Is for Adam
by Ken and Mally Ham
(Green Forest, AR: Master Books, 1994), 120 pgs.

D Is for Dinosaur
by Ken and Mally Ham
(Green Forest, AR: Master Books, 1991), 124 pgs.

Noah's Ark and the Great Flood
by Gloria Clanin
(Green Forest, AR: Master Books, 1996), 32 pgs.

The Tower of Babel
by Gloria Clanin
(Green Forest, AR: Master Books, 1996), 32 pgs.